INSTANT AIN'T EVERYTHING

Profitable Legacy Building Comes Over Time

CLAUDETTE REDIC

Published by Inspired4 U Publications
www.howtoselfpublishinexcellence.com

ISBN-10: 1543098010
ISBN-13: 978-1543098013

Change will occur for me when I change what I do.

– Claudette Redic

"Mom has been a great model to me and she has shown me how to give with elegance and ease. Her beliefs in the strength of God, our family and community have guided many of my life's choices."

— Claudette Redic

DEDICATION

To My Earth Mother, Doris Redic-Dickens, "Yes, I chose you." You have shown me by example, the importance of family and trust in God.

To Lucy Lorraine Bass Givens (5/21/1930 – 9/20/2014), you were an angel to all people. Regardless of the situation, we knew that Lucy loved us. She shared her unconditional love with all.

To Rev. Dr. Johnnie Colemon (2/18/1920 – 12/23/2014), you were my Spiritual Mother. You taught me everlasting universal 'New Thought' principles and how they are available to all.

To Janine A. Ingram, Life Coach, Mentor, Teacher, Guide and Co-Founder of 'The Love Journey, Inc., thank you for the inspirational experience within a sacred community that you provide every Monday through Friday. You continue to offer tools that enable each of us to take *action* on our dreams. Learning to love, appreciate, accept and forgive ourselves is the healing prescription you promote and live by.

To my son, Paul Roddy-Redic, you are my greatest pride. Your self-mastery, love and care for me and others are fulfilling and rewarding to witness and experience. I love you, Paul.

To my family,

The Men: I see what 'Good men do'. My dad, Monroe Redic, and my brothers, William, Monroe Leon (12/30/1948 - 6/9/1963), David, Dennis and Marvin, protected, encouraged, corrected and allowed me my own voice. I love you!

My Nephews and Great-Nephews: You are creative and loving. You regally demonstrate the possibilities for black young men of talent and purpose.

My Nieces: Erica, Adinah, Shevonn, Kayla, Ariel and Ariana, you *Black Girls Rock* and rule! I am extremely proud of you all.

CONTENTS

Acknowledgments   i

Foreword   vii

Preface   xi

1   Introduction   1

2   Harness the Energy: Ideas are wealth   3

3   Entrepreneurship: Serial Startups Are Possible   7

4   Celebrations: My Failures Count Too   15

5   Authors: Our Stories Are Important   27

6   Sources of Help: Collaboration Increases Relationship   35

7   Life Experience Empowers: I know That I Know What I Know   43

8   My Favorite Motivational Statements   63

About The Author   65

Sister-Friends (A visualization excerpt of Sistah's Home)   69

I Give Thanks and Praise to the Most High God for all He's done for me.

– Claudette Redic

ACKNOWLEDGMENTS

There have been a great number of supporters and living examples of success who have helped me complete "Instant Ain't Everything: Profitable Legacy Building Comes Over Time." I thank each of you who have offered words of encouragement and motivation to tell my story. You strengthen my commitment to build *Sistah's Home – The Place of Love in Action!* in Chicago, Illinois and make the manifestation of my vision more real.

Special thanks to Minister Jo Anne Meekins. Her excellent editing and publishing skills are only superseded by my appreciation for her patience, kindness and words of assurance. She kept me focused and empowered me to 'do' the work necessary.

Thank you author Navi of Northshore Publishing for my 'popping' book cover based on the original works of Spike Rebel and his autographed sketch of the "Queen Hostess".

To my 'ride or die' Sistah-Friends, Jacqueline Pinegar, Belinda Harris and Joy Sigur, who believe in me and create for me what Rev. Dr. Johnnie Colemon so succinctly described, *"A place where people have trusted me all the way to be whatever I said."* I love you and continue to offer the same space for you.

To my spiritual family, The Love Journey Inc, founded and facilitated by Life Coach Janine Ann Ingram, I love each of you. You make it clear that every reason for not having success is self-imposed. It is through my participation within this community that I get to experience the truth of what Barbara Stanny said in her book, *Over Coming Under Earning: A Five-Step Plan To A Richer Life,* that "the chief want in life is somebody who shall make us do what we can." Thank you for pushing, prodding and pulling me through!

To my family of friends who offer me their homes as my own, I love you! Your warm and loving welcome is what an open door of hospitality is supposed to feel like. Your unlimited and unconditional acceptance of me will be valued and appreciated forever. Thank you, Teresa and Carl Johnson, Yvette Maurice, Earline Hill and Felsie Woods, for maintaining a beautiful space for my visits. Your gift for creating a cozy and comfortable 'feel at home' environment is exactly what I want to develop and provide for the women who decide to visit *Sistah's Home – The Place of Love in Action!*

To the 'Way-Shower Women', you have made a way for many to benefit from personal dreams. Thanks for allowing me the privilege of 'up close and personal' experiences in your presence: Lillie Sanders, Dee Ingram, Carol Adams, Dee Alexander, Jamika Smith, Patricia Rich, Bertha Smith, Rev. Mildred Falls Davis, Sally Johnson, Josephine Wade, Gladys Scott, Lillie C. Rollins, Mildred Dixon, and Gloria Woodson.

To my Technology Friends and Associates, the tools you provided offered instant application opportunities. I thank you for the "*university of modern business processes and practices*" you have so freely given me:

Orin A. Fraser, my personal IT guru, gives me advice, equipment and technical answers where and when I need them most.

Rhea L. Steele and Brian Powers of Blue Ocean Logic continue to provide workshops of quality information along with major business support.

Tina James of Greater Southwest

Development Corporation demonstrates the power and importance of community input.

Sunshine Enterprises' Shelby Parchman, Ethan Daly and Ryan Pederson offered 'real-time' simulations of the business cycle.

Joel Hamernick and Rising Tide Capital offered community-based business development and accelerated training that can leverage access to capital.

The City of Chicago Small Business Center has tremendously contributed to my knowledge of support services and requirements to operate a business here.

My newest partner, the Building Our Prosperity (BOP) Business Center, is the evidence of successful collaborative works. Founder, Ro Davis and members are actively building sustainable communities and economic growth fostering generational wealth. Project 5000 opens its doors to the community adopting Dr. Webb Evans' principals, "Buy Black, Love Black and Give Black," to solidify African-American socioeconomic well-being.

To the Community focused organizations,

thank you for allowing me to partner with you in the services you provide our communities:

- National Block Club University– Syron Smith
- The Chicago Inventors Organization– Calvin Flowers
- The Black Star Project– Phillip Jackson
- Teena's Legacy– Jamika Smith
- The Global Girls, Inc.– Marvenetta Penn
- The Melody of Joy Institute– Joy Sigur Ramza.

Give yourself to yourself!

– Peggy Riggins

FOREWORD

Vibrant indigo, beautiful shades of purple and crimson in tow, she reminds me of sprinkles of gold with tinsel all about. A picture of her wouldn't be complete without a few sequins and taffeta with an organza overlay. I think of Cherry blossoms permeating the air on Sunday; and on Friday, a little patchouli greets your senses with a fine welcome. Claudette is a sister who swoons when she holds a baby because she always needs that 'baby love' as she calls it. Our elders love her because of her tenacity, energy and dedication to their comfort. She is 'Wombman' and an instrument of love and joy. I have witnessed her vulnerabilities that humble her and her strengths that increase her resolve to flourish without boundaries.

I remember first meeting my sister where we both worked. We hit it off immediately! She had an infectious smile that would invade your mundane day and infuse you with hope and excitement. Soon after, we were in lawn chairs on a beautiful afternoon at a jazz concert that she got free tickets for or on her back porch barbecuing because she adores good cuisine and comfort. She always seemed to be gifted with one ticket or another, so I hung around her in hopes that some of it could rub off on me... Well, that and the fact that she made me think, smile, laugh, reflect and feel deeper about life. When she is immersed in the rhythm of the drums, horn, guitar, piano and vocals, she is in her element. To watch her groove right in the middle of the dance floor is something to see. It makes me smile and then join in!

Her love for nature is only equal to her love for life. She loves her family like no other person I have met. Mother Redic is so blessed to have a daughter like Claudette, as she may get weary, but never worn. Her love and adoration for the Creator is a personal love that shows in her conversation and relationship with others. It is very evident how much she is loved and respected by her friends and family. My sister has instilled in me the philosophy that not all fights are worth my energy for a battle, but there are some fights that are worthy of being fought to the finish.

With a love for her people and *wombmen* around the planet, she has created a home for them. Sistah's Home – A Place of Love in Action! **will be** that place where *wombmen* can receive a much needed respite from life's issues and bring their overwhelmed souls to for healing. No matter where she comes from or where she is headed, a sister can find a hug, an ear, a shoulder and a meal at Sistah's Home as needed. Its elixir is the remedy. If you can heal a *wombman*, you will heal a nation because we are the first teachers of life and love and peace. Claudette's dream of Sistah's Home will very soon manifest into reality and I will be right there cheering with her, filled with pride in my heart for her. I can foresee warm happy tears flowing down my cheeks watching her dream became a reality.

Goddess/Queen/Mother/Sister Claudette! You are a *wombman* of great character, standards and a beautiful spirit. I am blessed to call you Sister-Friend! I love you very much!

Dear Reader,

Congratulations on being the recipient of this phenomenal piece of literature. It is my belief that it will enrich your life in a way that is evident in your future thinking and doing.

– Angela Wright

NOTE: Angela Wright is a 'younger sister' to me, a former colleague in the insurance industry, a dental hygienist, Yoruba priestess, aspiring Master Herbalist, mother and grandmother, spoken word artist, jewelry maker, accomplished sketch artist, and a poet. She loves being in nature and traveling. She has supported me in the vision of 'Sistah's Home' with untold hours of imaging and conversation along with the poetry and sketches of contributions she will make.

PREFACE

Nearly six years have passed since I was *released* from my job in corporate America's insurance industry. Despite my surprise of them letting a "valuable and trusted" Information Specialist go, I also experienced an internal sigh of relief. I reacted to the emotion of the moment, punching my fist high enough in the air that the 'terminator' signaled for her support people to move in closer. Freedom was at hand, but at that time, I had no specific plan for optimizing it in my life.

One of my first clues about my future came during the cab ride home with file upon file of non-policy related personal information about my client interactions with the company. I had earned accolades for my client interactions and had developed personal relationships with many of those clients, including the state and city of Chicago employees who had advocates and others working expeditiously for payment of their claims. I also took special interest and actions in working with small and independently-owned suppliers for the insurer. Knowing that their timely payments were perhaps more important to their business survival than it would be for the state or city per se, I made sure their accounts were reconciled with the same, and at times, more care in servicing. Those same files showed me how my attention to detail and quality of care for the clients could result in substance for me.

I took a panoramic view around me and saw that a large group of people, age fifty-five and over, were being released from the work force. Most had held middle-income jobs that allowed enough financial freedom to support even their extended families. They were being 'let go' without any real acknowledgement of their significant contributions or consideration for their obligations. During that time, most of us were thinking that our pensions and retirement income were not nearly enough to sustain our former lifestyle. I sat down and estimated the duration of my assets, which were completely gone within five years.

In retrospect, those five years moving through that wilderness were precious. I devised a plan to coach entrepreneurs to achieve their goals and obtain financial gains by utilizing a strong network of business partners to assist in the process. The solitude of the wilderness also returned me to my great love of *reading*. I later introduced a concept to create the now four-year old Cider Enterprises Book Club. This monthly conference call features authors who are *overcomers*. They are people who have been through the 'fires of life' and can now share their stories with love and hope in powerful ways that enlighten others.

That same wilderness period had plenty of un-welcomed aspects too. I encountered numerous spaces that proved to be uncomfortable, which was probably due to issues such as age, sex and unstated intentions. After being fed up long ago with various uncomfortable places and spaces, I made a non-negotiable commitment to myself: *I will not stay where I am not celebrated*. Experience showed me that when necessary, I could create a valued space for myself and the idea of *Sistah's Home – The Place of Love in Action!* was birthed from my commitment. With the generosity of supporters and investors who see and believe in me and my vision, it is my intention to create an opulent, engaging, warm and welcoming resort space that is in tribute to African-American women. It is a global destination that is family-friendly and grounded in *Hospitality*, *Hope* and *Health*. Sistah's Home invites the humanity of *Love* to be *in Action*.

The time for my lifestyle as a Queen is now. How do I know that it is now, you may ask? My resounding answer is: *At no other time in my life have the purpose, the possibilities and the forward-moving plans been more in alignment with who I am. Believe me, it has taken most of my lifetime to be at one with who the Creator made me to BE. I am the 'everything' I have been seeking and creating along the way.*

My only son, Paul, has a plaque on the wall in his home with this quote by Soren Kierkegaard – *"Life can only be understood backwards; but it must be lived forwards."* That gives credence to my foundational story that "Instant Ain't Everything." It took until now for me to understand and accept that most of my life experiences have generally translated into profitable business ventures. My 'voice of thunder' has been instrumental in attracting others to me. Creating and participating in learning adventures throughout my life have provided me numerous untold opportunities to explore relationships. My desire to always help others and my natural propensity to 'order things' led me to diverse groups of people, teaching me to adapt to outcomes that favored more than just my own successes.

Journey with me down *my* road to discover with certainty that "Instant Ain't Everything: Profitable Legacy Building Comes Over Time."

Rich people make decisions quickly and then they make the decision right.

– Black Cards Seminar

Chapter One

INTRODUCTION

The value I see in who I am, what I believe and what I do was not instantly attained. For years, the only thing instantaneous about me was self-judgment that immediately left me feeling inadequate.

So many ingredients have gone into creating the Queen I can now see in myself. Believe me; I have traveled many lengthy pathways before accepting my crown. Perhaps the first pathway was created while I was growing from a curious and energetic young girl surrounded by my family of five brothers, mom and dad, and at times, my paternal and maternal grandparents.

Today, as Queen Hostess, I am clear that I embody my purpose. I help harness the energy of ideas that produce profitable results. I use the gift primarily with entrepreneurs, yet there is more than enough room to pursue similar results in my community and personal family. I can see in the strength and 'breadth' of my networking that I am building powerful relationships with other business decision-makers. They are all people who believe that our collaborations are the solution to many shared concerns.

Claudette Redic – Cider Enterprises is my brand. I enjoy and appreciate this phenomenal lifestyle that allows me the freedom to focus on the three areas of my dreams and desires that fulfill me. These ventures of mine also put my claim and purpose to the test. Can I harness the energy of my own ideas and create profitable businesses? "Yes, I Can!" is my *instant* response. In having made this decision, I know that *everything* I do towards building a profitable business legacy is confirmation that I have made the right decision.

Chapter Two

HARNESS THE ENERGY: IDEAS ARE WEALTH

At the age of three, I could read. I remember it well because it became my joy to have my eldest brother, Pee Wee (William), listen to me read out loud. He was always patient and attentive to me and it was he who encouraged me to read to my other brothers. Mom gave birth to six children and I am the only girl. In my earliest memories, my older brothers covered me and it became my responsibility to cover my three younger brothers. Growing up in a household with a lot of male energy undoubtedly influenced a lot of my activities and actions early on. I received 'up-close and personal' training from the men

I recognize my natural attraction today to people who actually *do something* about things as opposed to just talking. Action was the order of the day. There was endless activity around feeding my brothers and preparing them for activities like school, sports, church attendance and prodding them to complete tasks assigned by our parents for the smooth running of our household. I was raised within a family that was quite specific about the roles and expectations for men and women. Even as a young girl, and most times, as the only other female at home besides Mom, I was expected to take care of the men's well-being. The males contributed their muscle and brawn to daily living. I still look to men today to do the heavy-lifting and provide the bravado when we're together. I intend to make them feel right at home in my presence.

My brothers were my earliest friends and I wanted to do everything they did. Until age ten, I was as loud, competitive and rambunctious as they were. I recall coming in from a baseball game with them and passing through the kitchen where the adults were. My paternal grandmother commented that I needed a bra on and her observation forever changed my ability to play with the boys. I was suddenly thrown into the role of a 'young lady' and expected to stay with the women and girls who to me, did nothing more than prepare for the men's needs. They centered their activities on things inside the home and their accompanying conversations were endless. It was in their presence that I learned I had a 'voice of thunder' that was too loud and opinionated. I was told, "Ladies do not speak out of turn or so loud."

Before I was ten years old, I was self-conscious about my body. I was the child giant in my grammar school pictures and even taller than some teachers. At ten, people certainly noticed me with my 36D bra size and 41 inch hips. I wouldn't describe myself as a big girl then. To me, it was more so that I developed early.

I wasn't called by my given name during my pre-teen years to mid-teen years. My family introduced me by age. "She's twelve, she's thirteen" and so on until I was about sixteen. Thank God I went off to college early and got to use Claudette all the time. Growing up, I was known as Necia, a nickname that family and folks from home still use.

Responsibility and big ideas came early in my life. I can remember at around age seven or eight, cooking a hot dog for Mom's lunch and adding her favorite Fritos and a Coke. I carried it across a major street to her at the beauty salon where she worked. That act of love was perhaps the start of the applause and accolades I would receive from others. I felt proud as they commented on my ability to cross a big street by myself and look after my mother's needs without being asked. I just knew Mom needed lunch about that time and I had 'playfully' learned how to cook eggs, hotdogs, and other simple sandwiches, so I fed her from that menu.

I took on more and more responsibility as my ideas and skills increased. Today, I am more selective in taking on responsibility since time has taught me that *to take responsibility is to take ownership.* The vigor and swiftness of saying "Yes" in my earlier years have evolved into careful consideration of the returns on my investments. Life experiences have made me very much aware of my time, my word, and my purpose. I can intuitively discern others intentions for my use in their lives. Even then, the biggest "No" they would get from me is when I see that I am more engaged in their success than they are. As much as I like helping others, I like it best when we are all actively working together for a predetermined end result.

Chapter Three

ENTREPRENEURSHIP: SERIAL STARTUPS ARE POSSIBLE

Many of my childhood experiences in entrepreneurship were a result of growing up as the daughter of the local beauty salon owner. For quite a few years, we were among the three black-owned businesses in our neighborhood. You know the mix– the grocery store, beauty salon and barber shop. I didn't count the church as a business back then. We lived within the LeClaire Courts projects on the southwest side of Chicago where our turf spanned the blocks from 43rd Street on the North to the South border of 45th Street. There might have been ten blocks between our East and West boundary. We were surrounded by white people and sometimes oppressed by their Jim Crow practices. Segregation was the Chicago way and in my mind, we only seemed to gain expansion in block-by-block increments. By the time my mother became owner of the salon, we had been allowed to move two whole blocks south, which put us on a main thoroughfare. Initially, there was little opposition to our business as we only served black people. But as time went on, racial hatred flared to the point where we children could only travel in packs for protection from neighborhood punks who thought it fun to egg us, our cars and storefront windows.

As we became teenagers, Mom set up an apartment in the back where we stayed until the last customer was finished and we went home together. My brothers and I had specific duties in the salon. My earliest assignment was to watch the kids while their parents received services. I loved playing with the children and created a routine that kept them busy and away from the adults. Soon after that, I started getting paid babysitting jobs. Mom allowed me to keep my earnings and I would hold on to my savings until I could purchase the things I wanted. I made sure I had more than enough for what I wanted because it was important for me to have money left over. I liked the idea of having money. It gave me something to hold over my brothers' heads. They seemed to always ask for a loan and I made sure they paid me back with interest.

Our community had a satisfying mosaic of services and activities that were managed by dedicated workers from city, religious and educational institutions. We had a selection of social programs that encouraged the arts, athletic programs that competed citywide and our local center offered industrial and life skills training. Ever the eager learner, I participated in everything. I had learned to sew from a cousin and used my budding skills to talk my way into making the skirts for our community-based drill team to wear in the famous Bud Biliken Parade. The success of that project paved another way for me to earn income throughout high-school and beyond.

During the latter sixties and after several years of ownership, our family-owned beauty shop expanded to include a boutique and a candy store. My job was to open and close the boutique, which was about the length of a hallway in distance from the salon. I liked the responsibility of being in charge and I learned how to prepare for running a smooth daily operation in every aspect. The cash register tapes and receipts were as important as the bathroom and fitting room. I tallied the daily receipts and was given the freedom and fun of creating arrangements that attracted purchases.

My hardest task was to keep my mouth shut from voicing my opinions. Mom avoided the usual beauty shop gossip by talking about fashion, doing something for others or just *shaking things up a bit* with a change to the traditional hairdo or makeup. It took but a few forceful slaps to my lips or my glasses being knocked to the floor before I embraced her message, "It's about the customer, not you." Those poignant memories influence me today in my personal commitment to satisfy the customer and serve from the mindset that the customer is always right. I sometimes have to self-motivate with the old adage, "The show must go on." And after pondering my bottom line for desired results and meandering through my personal feelings about whatever the situation, I conclude and once again confirm that nothing should interfere with customer satisfaction.

Negotiation integrity became a non-negotiable quality around that same time. Many of our boutique items were provided on consignment from Jewish merchants who required us to make weekly payments. When the salon was closed on Mondays, Mom would go make her boutique selections. It was my job, accompanied by several brothers, to go pay the merchants later in the week. Sometimes our payment would be *short* and it would be my job to get the merchant to accept a partial payment. I made up lies because of my shame and anger at having to do this and then I would have to remember to share the lie with the others in case the person mentioned it in another conversation. After I learned to stop lying and *hit people with the truth*, my negotiating skills really flourished. My ideas and imagination usually generated a few options to present that produced more favorable results for both sides. Operating in integrity eliminated my feelings of shame and anger. It is still my preference to know the truth even if it is painful.

I have long held to the notion that anyone can make *more* by simply doing *something* with what they have *at hand*. My constant flow of ideas kept me actively looking for ways to do just that. Basic skills, such as cooking, became a revenue stream for me in college. I had been responsible for the signature on family documents for so long that absolutely nobody challenged me. I moved out of the dormitory by forging Mom's permission and was the first one in my group to have my own apartment, where students paid me to cook their *favorites*. Outside of dorm food, only a few alternatives existed unless you had a car to get you there. The guys wanted steak and potatoes, and the women enjoyed making sweets at my place. I operated this 'irregular' restaurant throughout my college years and was royally compensated. Occasionally, I could also count on 'hotel' money from friends seeking privacy for short periods of time. During these rentals, I would either go visit a friend on campus or go home to Chicago for the weekend. I also wrote and edited papers for students and (sssshhh) I sometimes took tests for them. This enterprise provided another steady income stream because I enjoyed writing and could cram for a test and get a B or better nearly every time.

I take personal pride in doing an excellent job thanks to the early teaching and example of Mrs. Gladys Scott. Ms. Scott, as we all called her, worked as site director for the Jane Addams Hull House. This once famous social settlement in Chicago was originally devoted to services for European immigrants, but our isolated community also benefted from the services. Ms. Scott was devoted to their mission of helping others and she used her talents and convictions to help us *project kids* drop the cynicism and understand the value in having our names associated with excellence. Ms. Scott was a dark-skinned, black woman with buck teeth, which caused many children to create unflattering nicknames for her. She personally demonstrated that color and looks were mere distractions in life and that it was our responsibility to have a standard of excellence for ourselves.

Today, one of my business mentors, Donna Smith-Bellinger, the 'Revenue Accelerator' and author of "You Lost Me @ Hello," has helped me to better define my target market. This knowledge gives me greater confidence in selecting clients for my entrepreneurial coaching business. Donna asked me the vital question, "Who pays you for what you do?" She helped me to *see* my ideal clients and with the consideration of my skills and experiences, I can identify the likely qualities of my potential clients.

First and foremost, my ideal clients are trying to help somebody else. They are usually business owners or operators who have been doing what they do over time and are seeking support in specific areas. They are decision makers and loyal to their service providers. They are learning new technologies for marketing and promoting their ideas and can see the benefit of working within my network of business experts.

My concepts and beliefs about the legacy-building aspects of entrepreneurship came over time with experience. My confidence and success has roots in the evaluation of my self-worth. I have grown by investing in and trusting my relationships with others. As a lifetime learner, I utilize mentors, coaches, training, and practices that lead me to greater personal growth and development.

Chapter Four

CELEBRATIONS: MY FAILURES COUNT TOO

Designing a Time

I like celebrations. They are generally occasions that bring people together within a space that is specially prepared for the event. There is usually music and often food. To me, these are but basic ingredients for a gathering. Time and life experience have shown me that the most important ingredient to take everywhere is a positive attitude.

As a young girl, I loved to help my Mom prepare for visitors. She inspired me to make it *pretty* and to be sure that the conversation focused on the guest. Being an extremely curious person, I looked forward to the stories and gladly searched the house for items that we thought the visitor would like. Visitors might be relatives, the local Pastor, the school teacher or customers stopping by. They were in addition to the 'regular extra friends', we six kids usually had around.

Our home has always been a meeting place for business decisions whether public or private. Although the reasons varied, the underlying basis for each visit was usually the need of support from the family. Owning the local beauty salon was a signal to others that we had influence and money. In our own way, my brothers and I bought into that perception and would often bring another child's plight or request to the attention of Mom. She worked hard to help us help others. Sometimes her solutions would require a personal sacrifice or, more accurately, a delay in something she had promised to do for us. Her agreement to help was usually accompanied with a biblical principle that reassured her, like *"It is better to give than receive."*

We grew up in an environment where change was expected and expected often. We hosted Bible studies, homework groups, and team, planning and club meetings. These were held in addition to the usual birthday, anniversary or home-going repasts.

Celebrations had a themed look which

was dependent on the occasion. Food followed the function of the moment and usually included something sweet. During a hard or busy time, your sweet treat might be just a jelly cake with a bit of coconut sprinkled on top. In better times, we provided homemade treats from the best preparers and cooks among our acquaintances. Music might start from recordings and invariably, someone would break out singing or playing their instrument. Today, my elation of live performances remains with me and music continues to fill my heart with a sense of satisfaction and pleasure. I tell friends, "If there is no man in my life, let me fill the vacuum with live music."

Creating Places for Celebration

As we grew older, celebrations moved outside of the home. During my teenage years, we had 'The Center' which became a dance hall two nights a week for those of us between the ages of 13 to 20. Motown and other major record labels were creating new music every week and 'The Center' was where that teenage energy could be expressed and supervised. I hadn't turned thirteen yet when we started our dance parties, so I had to appeal to the kindness of Ms. Scott, the site Director. She made room for me even though she knew I was thirteen months younger than my brother Monroe who could come to the sock hops legitimately. I was taller and as fully developed as any young adult woman; plus my fast tongue and glib comments gave her a sense of my increasing maturity. I was quicker on my feet, but Monroe (aka Mose) had the charm. The two of us practiced our steps at home and would gladly be the first on the dance floor.

Our 'Center' became notable throughout the city as we began bringing in radio personalities. Famous DJ Herb Kent brought all the latest music and offers from advertisers. The famed "Soul Train" started in downtown Chicago and a number of us from 'The Center' were encouraged to go to the local television station and participate. I fondly look back over the sweat and creativity we poured into our 'rhythmic stroll' down the line. We were the definition of *cool*. My attention to fashion and sewing skills helped each outfit we wore represent our imagination of what *cool* looked like. We proudly strutted through the double row of other dancers, grooving to the beats while moving up the line for their turn to showcase their moves.

I learned about jazz clubs during those teen years too. Sundays in Chicago offered matinees with some of the greatest jazz performers in the world. At sixteen, I had the freedom to decide my after-church activities as long as I observed my curfew. That presented no problem for me since I was often perceived as the obedient daughter and seldom questioned. At the jazz sets, nobody ever asked me for identification so I made myself comfortable and gratefully took a seat up front. My soul resonated with the music. Every part of me was one with the music and I felt complete. My appreciation was demonstrated by uninhibited finger snaps and claps throughout the performances. Many times, while learning to curtail some of my natural enthusiasm, I had to allow my third finger to heal from the cuts caused by such forceful finger-popping.

By my late teens, my love for celebrating came to include cultural events in addition to dance parties. I had left the projects and gone to college. The Black Power Movement was gathering strength and the speakers from every 'thought perspective' were drawing nationwide attention. Coming from the political town of Chicago, there was an abundant selection of influences to support. I attended the meetings that introduced me to new and diverse people who were ready to take action on their beliefs. Always one to express my opinions, the movement gave me courage and a voice to do so with the people around me. I learned techniques and strategies that serve me to this day in recruiting like minds to do something. I basked in the period of the *Revolution* because even when we experienced systemic efforts to devalue our causes, we continued to celebrate our achievements.

The assassination deaths of President John F. Kennedy, Dr. Martin Luther King and Attorney General Robert F. Kennedy created a veil of grief across the nation for a long time. Many years passed without the lawlessness America began to demonstrate even to public figures. The riots within major cities personified black people's feelings of unrest and unfairness. Later, the order to open fire on those expressing civil disobedience during the infamous National Democratic Convention in Chicago convinced the *warriors* that our opposition to existing authorities carried real threats to our lives. For a long time, it seemed the only celebrations were the home-going services of the departed.

During the *Revolution*, my entrepreneurship ventures included multilevel marketing of health and nutrition supplements. I hosted weekly recruiting events that I moved across the city. The majority were held in a rented or donated room of the motel near my home. I used the value of music, beautiful and gracious women, along with Home and Garden hors d'oeuvres to set the stage for selling my male enhancement products. This was before Viagra and other products came out. The persuasive stories contained in the marketing information resulted in record sales that won me a trip to California.

That trip to California turned into another life-changing experience. I loved California on sight. Winning the trip brought me to the Bay area in July. San Francisco had the air of a big city and the ocean, my soul body of water, was a perfect place for me. But it was so cold, I sent home to Chicago for a fur coat to traverse the many wonders of the city. My love of maps inspired me to advance check the distance to visit my cousins. Thank God visiting them in the hills of Oakland gave me another enjoyable view of California that was much warmer. Lake Merrit gave me peace as I circled around it during my daily walks. I arose each morning to see my cousins off to work and shortly after, blasted their 'state of the art' stereo system from the top of those hills. The song of the day was "Zoom" by the Commodores.

My thoughts and map led me further down the coast to sunny Los Angeles. The warm sun was my hook. I stayed with lifetime sister-friend Jacqueline and her children. During my three days there, I decided to live in California. I found a great job in payroll at an oil refinery within the first day of looking. On day two, an apartment manager accepted my word and occupancy request to return in thirty days. Day three was filled with live music. We were in and out of places that seemed to have recording artists everywhere. Once again, live music helped me to feel alive and enthusiastic about life, and not give in to the vacuum of being alone. I seldom felt out of place in its presence.

I returned to Chicago and made my exit within the allotted thirty days. The next twelve years gave me time to gather more life experiences. My earliest celebrations in California were for the job I had landed. The refinery hired me at the expense of eliminating three good *white* workers. There was considerable angst around my being there. I was the first black and the first woman in such a position. At that time, foremen from all the areas would bring in about five hundred daily time cards and sheets. For years, several men had been doing the tally and record keeping. Well I, speedy and orderly with an affinity to patterns, completed their combined jobs with spare time to read a book afterward. Of course spare time was not appreciated so management added the busy task of dispatcher to my responsibilities.

Part of my job as dispatcher required me to notify the various departments of their celebration reward whenever they met safety goals. The planning and preparation was fairly simple since the celebrations were only a half hour long. I felt each occasion should be themed to reflect each department and consulted the workers themselves. Being typical men, most wanted food and fun. Humor became the keynote of all themes and I pleasantly discovered the men had talent. It wasn't long before my themed social events gained appreciation by the men. Welders, pipefitters and carpenters gave me most of the materials, and an accountant or chemist made an occasional contribution.

The created fun expanded to after work events. Being single with my own two-bedroom apartment, provided another space to celebrate. I felt comfortable among the male energy in the new environment having grown up in a house full of men. I knew not to become involved with co-workers in a romantic way, so our encounters were for games, gambling and groceries only. The guys came to accept me as "another one who got away." Many of the friendships I developed were with avid hunters, fishers and farmers. I received so many gifts I ended up establishing an exchange place that led to another unplanned, but profitable entrepreneurial experience.

For a long time while living in California, multiple income streams made me feel like everything I touched turned to gold. One of those income streams got me *up close and personal* with drug people and their money. The sight of money lined up in stacks the length of a double sized motor home was deeply impressive. I used my friendship with the people running the ring to give myself permission to *invest*. I won't bore you with the degradation I experienced with that bad decision, but I will tell you that remembering that tragic time allowed me to appreciate the *true value* in celebrations.

The freedom to appreciate the people you're with, the good feelings their presence brings and the simplicity and beauty of communing together is the foremost cause for a grand occasion. I left California with the blessings of sobriety, money from the sales of housing investments and enough severance pay with benefits to begin life again in another new location.

Today, whenever I create or support an event, I keep the purpose of celebration uppermost in my thoughts. If I fall into a lack mindset, which may include feelings of doubt or fear regarding any decisions to be made, I get still and wait for my answer. I can then shift into feelings of gratitude, victory, salvation and joyous appreciation. These are the ones I experience as I feel the hand of God working for my good. These are the ones that lead me away from and through any hell I have had in my life. That's reason enough for me to celebrate.

Chapter Five

AUTHORS: OUR STORIES ARE IMPORTANT

Nina Simone's music has always been inspirational and empowering to me. Her body of work, both musically and personally, offered a dominant background sound to many of my life experiences. Throughout this book, I share how some of her song-themes influenced me.

"I Wish I Knew How It Would Feel To Be Free" — Nina Simone

My very first paycheck came from the Chicago Public Library. I was the book attendant aboard the Book Mobile that made weekly visits to my underserved community. To this day, I have a special affinity for libraries. They are depositories of the exciting and unknown. They provide me information about people, places and things. It was the stories and studies that gave me a broad view on the perspective of freedom. A book contains the ability to transport me to another realm in just a few pages or it may allow me to attain a different and sometimes unimaginable state of mind by vicariously walking in the footsteps of a character.

In the days before the internet, the card catalog was my Google search engine. I could easily get lost in a new topic. As the Book Attendant, I was given permission to explore anything after my job of checking all the materials in and out from the daily line-up of readers was completed. The library was where my formal love affair with information and where to find it began.

In my earliest dreams about the freedom to live beyond my own life experiences, I inhaled stories about different places. I hadn't yet formed an opinion that living in the 'projects' was lacking in any way, yet the very idea of seeing and being in a different place was exciting. I loved the stories that gave descriptive details of daily life for families. Book series such as "Little Women" by Louisa May Alcott and Jane Austen's books were among my early favorites. At the time, I was not aware of black authors beyond the few mentioned during Black History month. Few stories were shared and we had none of those books at the school library or on the Book Mobile.

I loved reading so much that I would often miss events, choosing to read more instead. Sometimes the compulsion was so intense I'd isolate myself from others until I finished the book. By the time the *Revolution* came along, there was an unprecedented and prolific period of black authors available to me. Back then, I began to host reading parties so that my crew and I could discuss the selected important works. We ran the gambit of authors from the past to the new *hood* stories that were later described as black exploitation. Those books had exciting covers that showed black people in provocative roles and everybody seemed to be draped in *bling*. These books were quite a change from my early reading materials.

My habit of literally reading everything developed early. My brothers often teased me about reading the ingredients on the cereal boxes just as much as I read the cartoons and offers promoted on the back.

Because of my love for words, I became

an avid speller and competed in statewide spelling bees several times during my elementary school years. But, I was in high school when I intentionally set out to increase my vocabulary. I wanted to use words to avenge the injustices of the times without actually *cussing* people out. I knew that even in my resentment and anger, I had to be respectful to the adults I encountered. Once I got to blasting away with my forceful voice and powerful vocabulary, most folks couldn't understand the conversation. They only knew I was *pissed* about something. The few physical fights in my lifetime all resulted from inappropriate touching. However, I have waged many wars with words. I could slay you and there'd be no coming back.

When I was old enough to attend literary events, I often took a few friends along with me and made a point of getting a handshake or an autographed copy from the featured author. It was important for me to listen as they shared personal things about their lives that weren't in the book. I needed the reassurance that they were ordinary human beings with a story to tell and I admired how they seemed to naturally enjoy the limelight.

I think I first considered the idea for the

Cider Enterprises Book Club Conference Call while recalling some of the presentations I attended. By the time of the Book Club's initial call four years ago, life did not allow me much time to sit and read a book uninterrupted.

As I explored available technology to create the conference call and research topics, I did not find anything out there that focused on my theme of *overcomers*. Many of my entrepreneurial clients were spending their time and money on self-improvement books at the time. My intention for the Cider Enterprises Book Club Conference Calls was to offer them another option for sustaining *hope* in their own endeavors. I searched and found willing authors within my network who told their stories with enlightening love from a myriad of perspectives.

I found one of my first authors in my social media and marketing coach, Minister Jo Anne Meekins. Jo Anne helped me to put together a promotional package that I could offer featured authors to maximize exposure prior to their appearance. She created value in the call by setting up a social media marketing cycle to help me build and grow our audience.

Some of the great authors who have been featured on the call are:

- Ernest Basim Abdullah– The Game of Life and How to Play It
- Helen L. Bevel– The Spiritual Significance of the 1965 Nonviolent Right-to-Vote Movement
- Wanda Jenkins-Clemons– "Kwami and Kids" Children's book series
- William M. Griggs– The Megalight Connection
- Carla L. Hawkins– Mama Never Told Me
- Rosa J. Hodge– I AM … Affirmations for the Living
- Charles Holt– Between Me & Dad
- Janine Ann Ingram– Born To Be Rich
- Naleighna Kai– Every Woman Needs A Wife
- Naleighna Kai & M-LAS– Baring It All: The Ins and Outs of Publishing
- Rev. Dr. Barbara King– Transform Your Life

- Asadah Kirkland– Beating Black Kids

- Valerie Love– The Christian Witch Theory

- Shelia McKeithen– Twelve Steps To Your Healing

- Jo Anne Meekins– Living a Vocal, Valued and Victorious Life series

- Kajara Nia Yaa Nebthet– "Light as a Feather" and "I Get Energy from the Sun."

- Susan D. Peters– Sweet Liberia: Lessons From The Coal Pot

- Peggy Riggins– You Taking Care of You

- Kathleen Y. Robinson– The Store Story

- Linda Yerby– Journey To Greatness

- V. Lynn Whitfield– The Party's Not Over Until God Says So

- Rev. Craig Wright– It All Adds Up

Thanks again to Jo Anne Meekins and her meticulous work! The recordings from the calls are archived and can be heard on the

Cider Enterprises YouTube Channel at www.youtube.com/c/ClaudetteRedic. My blog also offers author enhancing articles and video highlights on the Author Showcase page at www.ciderenterprisesbookclub.com.

In sharing their stories, every one of our featured authors seemed to free themselves to do even greater with their lives. I follow many of them online and see them working on other big projects in their everyday lives. They remain bright stars and shining examples as we, the readers, get the overflow. The joy my *overcomer authors* express is contagious and I am so honored to have had them share their stories. They are my encouragers in getting my own story out to the world.

Keeping a place for Authors in my life will be a manifested centerpiece of the Hope Pavilion, the space designed for book lovers within *Sistah's Home – The Place of Love in Action!*

Chapter Six

SOURCES OF HELP: COLLABORATION INCREASES RELATIONSHIPS

Why I Collaborate with Others

1. I do not exist alone in the world. My intention is to help others. Collaboration is probably one of the easiest ways to do that. The start of any collective work is to get to know 'Who' wants help. Experience developed over time has proven that I first need to cultivate a relationship with them. Even in my experience with the least of them (children and other marginalized groups), I had to get to know them before asking if and how I could help them.

I recall an experience when I was working to support a young girls group that we adults decided needed us as mentors and guides in their development We gathered materials, plenty of food for our once-a-month gatherings and created what we considered an exciting and important mission statement and program. The girls came initially, but seemed to enjoy the food most. After a while, even the food was not enough to stabilize our number of attendees. During this period when it seemed we would lose the remaining girls due to lack of interest and commitment, I happened to meet a young girl. This girl became my protégé. She had that *can do spirit* and said she liked me. Yes, I received the compliment and asked, "Why do you like me, someone you only see occasionally?" In her own way, she wisely responded, "I like how you are always happy and talking about a good time you recently had." She mentioned how I allowed children to express their opinions and paid attention to their answers. She also liked that I had time to spend with children.

I soon invited her to join our group of mentees and talked to a director in the program about her. When the director met her, she officially asked her to come aboard. The child *blew us away* when she asked, "Why would I want to be a part of your group? What does it offer that I like to do?" We were blown away because we had never considered asking any of the girls what we could do for them. We had great ideas, but no real relationship with the girls we wanted to help. This lesson from one so young reminded me to establish a relationship that begins from a place of genuine interest in knowing another human being. This is the important first step to building strong collaborations.

2. I am a decision maker and collaborating with others has helped me achieve my goals sooner than later. My most successful collaborations were achieved when I developed an understanding and various ways of responding to the communication style of the other collaborator. I had to literally *hear* how they talked about issues and identify if they were they the big talkers who were able to provide written documents to substantiate their claims or if they were the ones who could show physical evidence without 'paper proof' of their worth. Some of my collaboration partners have been ones to

give the go-ahead signal for us to work together with a nod of their head.

Hearing and responding to and in the communication style of the collaborative partner facilitates the likelihood of a strong relationship. Collaboration is an Art. The initial canvas for the desired result is most times blank. Even though the first contact may have been initiated by referrals, references or research, the contributing artists generally discuss an expected outcome. Life experience helps greatly in this area and listening is the key.

I have spent considerable time showing off what I know and overselling myself. I was working way too hard to convince someone to work with me. I admit that I spent a huge amount of time locked in my ego of knowing what's best for everyone involved. It was really a form of control I thought I needed to exercise in a relationship. Time has thankfully revealed to me the importance of hearing with more than my ears.

3. Building *Sistah's Home – The Place of Love in Action!* will be extraordinary proof of my

mastery in the art of collaboration. Going forward, my ability to attract the people I need to participate in its manifestation is vitally important. My relationships and their purpose are far reaching in range and complexity. I measure the strength of them by their ability to convey the foundational concept of hospitality, hope and health. I would say that real success can be assessed with the willing contribution of time and money to build and sustain Sistah's Home.

My motivation to proceed is largely influenced by my reflections on the path of my manifested dreams and desires during this journey. In recalling one seemingly impossible moment in my life, I am encouraged that all things are possible and I can have the desires of my heart.

One of my serial entrepreneur experiences involved me moving to a new city to introduce the new concept of nail care in a salon. I was inspired to go into the nail business because nail shops existed on nearly every corner in California, but in Memphis, I couldn't even get my own nails done. I thought creating and promoting the concept of consistent nail care could provide a service for others and provide great revenue for me. My first significant collaboration came from the local manicurist. She told me she had done manicures in her home for many years and men were her largest group of regulars. Generally, these men worked in executive or sales positions. She said there was a market for women, but she had determined that "women wanted too much" and she was satisfied with the men's handsome tips and the simplicity of their service requirements.

My ambitious plans to change things began to gain traction after learning the *southern way* of doing business. Very few women had businesses outside the home during that time. Men were the business owners and women needed a *male covering* to operate. Here I was, a newly relocated black woman wanting to operate in an industry that was still stuck on giving services within color lines only. Fortunately for me, I had plenty of male cousins and a big brother living there who smoothed the way for my sole proprietorship.

The local school of cosmetology had a manicuring program that allowed licensing, but enrollment was contingent upon a male barber's recommendation. Well again, I had just the right male barbering cousin. It took several more small collaborative relationships for me to open a shop inside a movie and game mall. The services of both a white and black beauty salon were available. In addition, there was a black and white barbershop. The four of them decided I was not in competition with them and could possibly be of service to their customers. Their decision led to a five-year relationship that enriched us all.

I am rich, prosperous, healthy and wealthy. I know that the grace of the Lord overflows for me.

— 1 Timothy 1:14

Chapter Seven

LIFE EXPERIENCE EMPOWERS: I KNOW THAT I KNOW WHAT I KNOW

I Know that Family is First

My mom tells the story of her concern about my father getting to John Gaston Hospital in Memphis, TN in time for my February 11th birth on a snowy, frigid night. She continues with a tale of going into another dimension during the time of delivery, but is fuzzy on the details. She said, "Wherever I had gone to, I felt I needed to get back to see what you, my third child and only daughter, were going to do." She doesn't say how long it took to work her way back to conscious living. Also, I don't recall her cuddling or comforting me during my early years.

Dad is the one I remember as the man who made things right. He probably set the stage for my early concepts of sovereignty.

He always gave me information about how to move forward with whatever life offered. I can't remember him ever criticizing me and he would tell me, "Don't be a baby! You can do it!" Till this day, the spirit of those words motivates many of my entrepreneurial endeavors, and still keeps me hopeful about the things that I can change.

Many people called my moneymaking activities *hustles* and for a long while I agreed with that term. But in college, my classes in finance and accounting gave me a new language. I became an *entrepreneur*. The Black Power Movement was a broad platform during that time and lent a renewed awareness to the reality of our own self-sufficiency. This was the climate I thrived in, the very environment I had been raised in. My voice became a loud horn proclaiming our ability to "get it for myself," as James Brown said in his song, "Open up the Door."

I had operated most of my ventures on a cash flow basis and it wasn't until many years later that I found out I was *poor*. I always had money for what I wanted, but in accordance to my financial understanding of today, I now look at it another way. Having a regular cash flow gave me enough money to conduct a fulfilling quality of life, but I did not use it create wealth. It was much later that I began to consider stocks, bonds and houses as my chosen means to accumulate long term wealth. I could see that owning a business was a great challenge on many levels but if done well, it would create wealth. That was where I focused my energy.

I Know I Give Life the 'Open Sesame' Command – I Can Have What I Want

Near the end of my twenties, I was looking for direction and a renewed purpose. I was experiencing career expansions and making money from my entrepreneurial investments housing visitors in California. That venture paid for two mortgages and allowed me to travel every six weeks. I made it a point to either go somewhere to see a new place or to replenish my inventory of the merchandise I sold to personal shoppers. I traveled abroad extensively from the late 60's until the mid 70's. Africa, Europe and the Caribbean Islands held my attention for a decade after leaving home. Once I began living and working in California, my trips became adventure-filled weekend excursions. I met people who had motor homes, enough camping gear for a compound, and who loved showing me the various landscapes of this magnificent state. I still anticipate resuming residence for several months of the year, one day.

I remember when I got my first house there. It had a little scraggly back yard. My first home improvements went into making it a pleasant place to be. I would eat breakfast and dinner outside so much that my neighbors, who never used their yards, started eating outside too. Soon we were taking turns with food preparations and decorations since we had children by then.

Despite the appearance of a great life, I felt a vacuum. Many of my relationships seemed to lack emotional depth. Most were superficial and only a few lent themselves to a feeling of lasting value. California was about images and it was there that I found the need to experience intimate relationships that would reveal much more than any surface encounters could provide. Family and friend gatherings were my natural way of engaging with people. I saw that my need for family had me creating connections with people who I came to call Cousin, Aunt Tee, and Brother. I did my *usual* with them and made sure we had plenty of occasions to get together. Family was critical to my deep need of belonging to more than the moment.

I Know that "The Beat Goes On," as in The Whispers' Song

My greatest purpose for being alive at thirty was to give birth to my son. This is one of those times when, as my Mom often says, "You know what you know." I experienced my greatest sense of relief as his head emerged from my body. The music in my soul had me literally rise up on the delivery table and sing lyrics from The Whispers' song aloud. "…and the beat goes on." In that moment, I knew for eternity that Paul and I would be just fine. The six people waiting in the 'family room' still laugh and tease me when they recall how I started singing before I even asked for my glasses!

During my joy-filled time of pregnancy, I asked myself "*What should I read to him first?*" It might seem silly, but where to lead his mind was important to me. I started with the Bible, especially after my decision to name him Paul. We spent many a nursing and nighttime hours reading together while rocking in my chair. I felt complete then and now. It was through motherhood that another expression of my purpose was clearly revealed.

I felt confident that I could provide a happy home for him even without a father in his life. I thought, "After all, I have brothers, uncles and cousins who dominate the family in numbers and can show him every aspect of being male." I had just a few expectations for my seemingly perfect, number one son:
1. We are not a statistic.
2. You must get an education.
3. No babies and no jail time on my watch.
4. Family is the place you can always go to, but you must help to make it a safe and sacred place.
5. We look to you to contribute to its success.

He said my expectations of him were too high.

I knew he honored and loved me for real when during one of my few chastisement sessions, he grabbed the extension cord and hugged me. I knew that he could have physically challenged me then, but he loved me into submission instead. We went through a period during his teen years when punishing him hurt me too. Travels and visits during school breaks became undeserved pleasures that caused me to enforce the "word of the parent" and sit it out. Being the enforcer was a job I preferred to allow the experts to handle as long as they followed my directions. We spent years together in California and Memphis until we ultimately returned to Chicago while Paul was in Junior High School. His J.H.S years were pivotal in our relationship.

I returned home to Chicago to work as a manicurist with women I already knew. I figured I could live okay with my abilities and a few add-ons, such as my personal shopping services and my tax preparer, insurance agent and notary skills. One day during a casual conversation while manicuring a client's nails, I was offered an opportunity to come and work with a new concept of support for entrepreneurial women. The World Bank would back the program and my job would be recruitment and maintenance of administrative records for the "Circles" that consisted of five women each. I had asked, *"What's next for me Lord?"* The Universe responded with what I had obviously been waiting and ready to receive because the next four years were consumed with "The Women's Self Employment Project."

Paul's high-school years occurred during a time of 'kids' clothing being stolen' and parent action. I moved from the hood to downtown Chicago for safety. Paul worked for the Chicago Bulls during three of their championship periods. He was greatly favored and received gifts from many sources. I allowed him to keep some gifts and others he could not. One of the 'could nots' was from an older woman closely affiliated with the Bulls who wanted him to have keys to her car and apartment. Paul's young age did not seem to a problem for her at all. Yes, Paul was responsible, respectful and thorough in following details, but he did not need that much freedom at sixteen. I wanted him to stay interested in sports and the guys, not the girls or women, just yet.

After his high-school years, we both moved to Atlanta. He was to attend school there and I was off to work with my brother Dennis in our new company that later licensed his 'Insert-A-Blind' invention. We believed we were setting up our legacy for generations to come, which drove us night and day for the next five years. It was certainly one of my most creative times in business. I gathered information about a whole new industry and was again able to attract the right people who helped us harness the many ideas needed to bring the product to market.

Meanwhile, Paul reunited with two friends from California and they set up their household. These three young men sharing their first independent living experience had their lives tragically changed when one was murdered as he answered the door. It is only many years later that I can see my son has finally *recovered* from his pain. He spent a decade 'chillin', drinking and, to me, killing himself before his change came. The sense of peace, inner joy, confidence and determination he had as a boy returned to him as a man! I praise God and *I know that I know* it was only His grace that brought my son back to life, loving the Lord. My admonition to parents is to not give up on your children or, more importantly, the work God can do in their lives. It is true, you can only save yourself. It's better to let go and ask God to work in your own life and supply whatever you need to hold love for your child. My mothering roots have yielded me great fruit, perhaps the greatest being forgiveness.

I Know that I Still Need Testosterone All Around Me

Another part of my life centers on Nina Simone's song, "You Don't Know What Love Is."

I confess to checking the recently added *never married* box on several official papers. I guess it's better than a 'spinster' box, which sounds so lonely. Even now, I wonder if I will ever know what love for a man is beyond the love for my son and brothers. I continue to use them as my measuring stick in my present unfulfilled desire to be in a life-long relationship with a 'Good Man'. Yes, I still desire to experience marriage. However, my three engagements and zero weddings cause me to wonder sometimes. I can honestly say I believe I felt love for the few men who have been a part of my life. It was my most recent beau that caused me to take a long reflective journey while he was enthusiastically exalting his value and worth to me.

My first serious romance was with an older friend of my brothers. He created and used my preference for a *slow hand* to win me over. He spent several years just being my friend and when we finally connected completely, I was hooked for years afterwards. Our pledged affections and promises of marriage changed when he went to Vietnam and I experienced college. We both found that we had changed too much to salvage our former relationship after he returned. However, I had to carry a revolver to convince him that I was through and that we were no longer a couple. At least ten years passed before we were able to resume our friendship. His parents called me their daughter-in-law until their death many years later. During his time of bereavement, I was there to hold him in his pain.

My longest boyfriend experience became an intimate all-consuming twelve-year relationship. Again, it all began with a great friendship. His world was so different from mine. We met as caseworkers for the State of Illinois. I was a part of the first large group of black caseworkers the state had ever hired. Most of us were recent graduates from local universities and colleges. We considered ourselves fortunate to become part of a system that helped our people and offered us benefits. He obtained his job through the political clout his family held.

My altruistic view countered his conviction that everything had a price and was negotiable. Our often strongly opposing opinions and mutual attraction as opposites gave us plenty of ground to cover in our time together. It didn't take long after becoming an official couple before we decided to *shack-up*. We moved in together amidst the controversy of my mom's objection and his parents' open and favorable acceptance of our arrangement. Over time, our lives as caseworkers reflected an appearance of unrelated opulence due to the procurement of *hot* items we acquired through our side hustle and unsavory relationships.

We held a place of attention in our community because we invariably had something going on all the time. We brought new "Fleetwoods" every year and alternated colors between black and white. We frequently hosted great celebrations and thought we had it 'goin on', and we did for a while. But, the sale and use of drugs threw us off our winning game as the power couple to know. His role in *the life* expanded until our once normal friendliness dissipated as he tried to hide the extent of his involvement. Near the end, the addiction forced my decision to save myself and literally go into hiding. At the time, it was hard to disappear from my busy life but divine providence prevailed again when I asked for help. It took two years to successfully relocate without him stalking me, my friends and of course, my family. At least 'ten thousand' experiences later, my *recovered* friend with the masterful mind, suave good looks and a wife was back among my regular associates. I like to believe we have both become better people because of our life experiences.

"Friendship first and then see how the relationship evolves from there" is an expectation I still maintain. Life experience has taught me that it is imperative to establish a high degree of integrity first while developing a friendship. I see men out there being wonderful *coverings* for their women and families. Rev. Ike says, "You're not going to get any more in life than what you can visualize" and so as I await my covering, I use his statement calling out what you want, "It is for me." I see and declare, "*My husband is on his way to me.*"

I Know that My Dream Knows Me

Nina Simone's song, "I Got Life," is another deeply interwoven part of my ancestral DNA. It fortifies my resolve to 'do it' (life) just as I am. I used this motivation when I decided to promote and start sharing my vision for building a place of opulence and abundance that offered relaxation and rejuvenation for black women. Sistah's Home – The Place of Love in Action! needed "Instant Ain't Everything" as its official call to action.

Now is when plans are being decided for the communities surrounding the biggest economic and tourist area on Chicago's South Side. In this historical racially segregated area, the forthcoming Obama Library will reside. Along with the contribution of the World Class Golf Course that Tiger Woods pledges to make and the additional visitors it will bring, we need to have our places of accommodation ready for the influx of people.

I Know that Claudette Redic and Cider Enterprises want a Seat at the Table

The question became, "Who, besides you, knows that you belong there?" It was then that I began to explore branding ideas and took an Archetype Quiz that helped me objectively conceptualize Claudette Redic.

My test results verified that "I Got Life" for sure. The personality test was based upon several theories of noted psychologist Carl Jung. I was in complete agreement with my results. In exploring the attributes of being a Queen, a Ruler, an Ambassador and a Sovereign personality type, I was more effective in selecting and creating my branding and marketing ideas.

The beauty of this new form of conceptualization was that it gave me language to describe my personal brand of ideas, people, and relationship networks. It offered visualization opportunities of the inner me. I could show my connections to the Universe.

In reflection, it is interesting to me that this information would present itself at the same time I was seeking answers to these questions: *Who am I now? What's my focus? Do I trust my gifts as more than enough to receive the riches God has promised to pour out for me?*

I Know that I Must Encourage and Remind Me of My Own Worth

MY COMMERCIAL

I am a Bold, Brave and Beautiful Woman! My radiant smile perfectly complements my 'voice of thunder'. My long, strong, sensuous arms embrace me, the Universe, and all life. Indeed, I am One with the One!

My very essence is Hospitality, Hope and Health. Oooh ... that sway of the ancestors' hips on me is uniquely designed to flow with the rhythms of life. Yes, my gift for harnessing the "energy and ideas" of businesses, organizations, and entrepreneurs distinguishes me as an outstanding Business Coach and Consultant.

My biggest dreams are realized as I, Claudette, move forward with assurance and confidence. Opulent Abundance surrounds me and I have many portfolios of great value that allow me financial freedom and independence. My greatest wealth is my belief and knowing that God is the Source of my supply. He is my "Instant Everything" and lifetime business partner.

My long legs are invariably dancing to the beat of my own inner music and my slender feet take me into action for my community. My lengthy toes curl in amazement at just how *Bad* I am.

My life as Claudette is filled to the overflow with love, peace and joy. Children, flowers, music and art provide me the opportunity to relax and release on a daily basis. And finally, my enthusiastic actions reveal that I am expecting my greatest good right now!

This is my commercial. Creating it was an assignment given to The Love Journey community by Founder, Janine Ingram. I needed to hear what I had to say about me and not the business, the baby, nor anything or anyone else, just me. After a number of trials, I got it. Who better than me, could tell me about me? I get to choose the language, the labels and the importance of my life. I get up in the morning greeting myself with a warm embrace and speaking aloud the words, "I love you, Claudette." I thank the creator for me and another day!

These practices have taken some time for me to comfortably do. I was a fully grown woman before I began to talk directly to myself. This was one of the most liberating personal feats I had taken on in some time. Yes, I'm always learning something new so this was a key step in my growth to become more and more attuned to what's going on within me. On reflection, I see that I do it so naturally for others, yet I had not considered the value in encouraging and uplifting myself. When I look in the mirror now, I see a person of worth, a good person and yes, a person who is loved.

These words of faith, life, power, wisdom, understanding, love, order, zeal, renunciation, surrender and trust are what I will use to tell my own story of being an *Overcomer*. I will use my commercial to keep myself on course, push through any resistance and move forward with unveiling my dream to the world... *"Sistah's Home"* – *the Place of Love in Action!*

It is only now that I can affirm and talk about the indescribable joy that I feel in the reality of being a life created by my God, the Most High. It's that joy that sets my drum beat, my rhythm, my message and my way. I am grateful to say I can now appreciate the multitude of puzzle pieces I Am. I embrace and reconcile my take charge behavior, my 'voice of thunder', my creation of hospitable spaces, my need for order, my desire to lead people to improvements, my love of information and my conviction in achievement. They all describe the multiplicity of my authentic self.

These natural multiplicities also provide me the vantage point to own and operate as Queen Hostess of *Sistah's Home – The Place of Love in Action!* My life experiences will help me continue to harness the energy of the best ideas that promote hospitality, hope and health. In this connected environment and movement of minds and spirits, we will build this 'made for us resort' right here in Chicago, Illinois as a tribute to African-American women. I have the best possible collection of life experiences to do this. This same collection assures and fortifies my conviction that "Instant Ain't Everything: Profitable Legacy Building Comes Over Time."

Remember, when you do not trust yourself, you cannot and will not trust anyone else. Instead, you will ignore your inner voice and intuitive inklings and tell yourself what you feel is wrong.

— Iyanla Vanzant

MY FAVORITE MOTIVATIONAL STATEMENTS

I share the affirmations, scriptures, statements and questions that motivate, inspire, encourage and assure me that I can have what I want, I can be who I want, and I can do what I want because *I Am One with The One.* I hope they will do the same for you.

- ❖ I am rich, prosperous, healthy and wealthy. I know that the grace of the Lord overflows for me. – 1 Timothy 1:14

- ❖ It works if you work it. – Rev. Dr. Johnnie Colemon

- ❖ Give yourself to yourself! – Peggy Riggins

- ❖ What you argue for you will have – Gerry Roberts' Black Cards Seminar

- ❖ Rich people make decisions quickly and then they make the decision right. – Black Cards Seminar

- ❖ Poor people make decisions slowly, and then they change them often. – Black Cards Seminar

❖ Most every reason for poverty and underearning is self-imposed. – Barbara Stanny

❖ Change will occur for me when I change what I do.

❖ What difference do I want to make before I leave this planet?

❖ What is the goal that translates into an emergence or the difference I want to make? – Michael Beckwith

❖ I don't want no rocks crying out in my place. – Rev. Paul Jones

I Give Thanks and Praise to the Most High God for all He's done for me.

Namaste,

Claudette Redic

ABOUT THE AUTHOR

Claudette Redic is the ageless founder and owner of Cider Enterprises, a business umbrella that includes coaching and consulting primarily for entrepreneurial women.  Cider Enterprises maximizes life experiences to harness the energy of ideas that produce profitable business ventures. The Cider Enterprises Book Club Conference Call component and Cider Enterprises consulting are the vision building foundation for *Sistah's Home – The Place of Love in Action!*

Cider Enterprises, (Redic spelled backwards) started as a family-owned business until Claudette became sole proprietor in 1985. Cider Enterprises has evolved from several retail and service operations into a lifestyle that Claudette uses to create, promote and support individualized business ventures. Global travels and the opportunity to live in several major cities within three states focused her attention on women with ventures that needed a broad canvas to paint their life stories upon. Most of these women wanted to help others and needed a community of support that assisted them with new technologies and current financial options. Today, a collaborative network of partnerships enables Cider Enterprises to be responsive to the individual needs of entrepreneurs. Clients have included sole proprietors, midsize corporations and nonprofit organizations. *"My lifetime goal is to work with other people who are willing to contribute their time and energy to create solutions for the issues at hand."*

Claudette, affectionately known as Queen Hostess, enjoys providing warm hospitality to people and is also the single mother of Paul, her wonderful adult son. She is the sister of brothers William Carter, Monroe (deceased), David, Dennis and Marvin Redic. They are her standard of measure for 'good men'. Very much alive today is her mom and anchor Doris Redic-Dickens. *"Mom has been a great model to me and she has shown me how to give with elegance and ease. Her beliefs in the strength of God, our family and community have guided many of my life's choices."*

Claudette is a lifelong-learner, who still takes classes, courses and workshops that help her make informed decisions. She has directed much of her work and words toward peaceful improvement. Claudette learned 'New Thought' and other practical solutions to live a better life, as a spiritual daughter of the late Rev. Johnnie Colemon of Christ Universal Temple.

"Instant Ain't Everything" shares Claudette's story of finding value in herself. It has also helped her assess and appreciate the many gifts and options she provides to help others. She can now clearly see that her purpose always contained instant responses and actions that she could readily utilize. Yet, it has been the analysis of those responses and actions that makes her everything she is today.

You can connect with Claudette at:

Email: Ciderenterprises@gmail.com

Web: www.ciderenterprisesbookclub.com; www.claudetteredic.com

Book Club: Every 3rd Thursday from September through April. Check to connect....

Facebook: www.facebook.com/AuthorsandBooksPromoter

LinkedIn: www.linkedin.com/in/claudette-redic-b6377425

What is the goal that translates into an emergence or the difference I want to make?

– Rev. Michael Beckwith

NOTE: *To clarify my vision of what Sistah's Home looked like and what happened there, I created fictional short stories of women and their experiences while visiting. The following is a visualization excerpt of several long-time sister-friends concluding their visit at Sistah's Home – The Place of Love in Action!*

SISTER-FRIENDS

Sunday morning dawns and the Sister-Friends meet in the chapel for the last time on this visit. They share a quiet meditative period together that symbolizes their oneness. Sister-Pastor, making the first move, leads them in prayer. Her prayers encompass the Sister-Friends, covering their families and concerns. "Namaste," they say affirming the divinity in each other after the prayer. Sister-Pastor unconsciously begins humming a soft melody of thanksgiving as the Sister-Friends quickly join voices and embellish the melody with lyrics.

After leaving the chapel, the Sister-Friends head directly for the spa area agreeing to revisit the former importance they gave to keeping their bodies physically fit. Sister-Speaker laughed saying, "My very livelihood in the public eye requires that I keep my 'gurls' high and my bottom tight. You know me, still dancing to every great beat and then some." They leisurely make their way to the top floor for one last look at the tranquil lake. Sister-Speaker takes time to make her final phone calls, arranging to pick up a week's worth of Chef Paul's nutritious and tasty home meals. She really appreciated not having to worry about this aspect of her life. Her schedule for the upcoming week was filled with a number of appearances and she had learned from past experiences to keep her food as light and natural as possible.

The Sister-Friends lovingly embraced as they prepared to leave the picture perfect view and sanctum that always stimulated a more peaceful and enlarged perspective of their lives. Sister-Pastor gave a prayer of continued blessings for each of the Sister-Friends. Then they firmly grabbed hands and circled around three times in both directions, first to the right and then to the left. They were filled with childlike glee that was similar to the high-spirited joy they experienced as young girls.

They concluded their sisterhood ritual and boisterously declared their affirmations of acceptance for themselves and each other: "We are Perfection in Expression!"

The Sister-Friends' luggage and other personal effects had been sent down earlier, so they headed back for a final toast in Queen Hostess' palatial quarters. After their last drink and more hugging, they headed for the private elevator and chatted about their next visit on the way down to the lobby. Each Sister-Friend personally thanked Queen Hostess again for the lovely visit. She responded in delight of having spent this precious time with her dear friends. Queen knew without a doubt that these wonderful women felt how much she valued and loved them, and would be in her life forever.

Sister-Pastor, always the first in everything, gets to the exit and exclaims "Oh, here comes my ride. I love the service at *Sistah's Home – The Place of Love in Action!* Even upon departure, they demonstrate quality service and the utmost care for their guests." Then she laughingly asks, "Queen, did you tell them to have my car come first or are they so familiar with guests' habits and preferences they just know when to take action?"

Sister-CEO Ellie radiantly emerges through the doors, sensing that others must see how well-rested and more confident she is than when she arrived. She is self-assured that her plan of action to assist Queen in leading the Cider Enterprises board and staff in wealth building is right on target. Ellie's bright eyes light up and her smile grows broader as she notices her shiny detailed car parked at the curb. She generously tips the polite young doorman, who courteously receives her ticket and escorts her outside. After she is safely seated, Ellie drives off. Her platinum grey Mercedes S550 4Matic effortlessly glides into traffic with a quiet purr.

Cowboy is next to approach the door to pick-up Sister-Speaker. Arm in arm, the two of them happily stroll away with a warm farewell and a fervent wave as they enter their car.

Well, until next visit!

****

Dearest Reader, we invite you to sow into the vision of **Sistah's Home - The Place of Love in Action** with your donation of any amount to the link below: www.paypal.me/ClaudetteRedic.